TIGHT CORNERS

By the same author

The Young Detectives Handbook
The Sherlock Holmes Challenge Book

W. V. BUTLER

TIGHT CORNERS

Puts you into forty tough spots . . .
and challenges you to spot the way
out!

Illustrated by Andrew Price

A DRAGON BOOK

GRANADA

London Toronto Sydney New York

Published by Granada Publishing Limited in 1982

ISBN 0 583 30517 2

A Dragon original
Copyright © W. V. Butler 1982

Granada Publishing Limited
Frogmore, St Albans, Herts AL2 2NF
and
36 Golden Square, London W1R 4AH
866 United Nations Plaza, New York, NY 10017, USA
117 York Street, Sydney, NSW 2000, Australia
100 Skyway Avenue, Rexdale, Ontario, M9W 3A6, Canada
61 Beach Road, Auckland, New Zealand

Printed and bound in Great Britain
by Cox and Wyman Ltd, Reading
Set in Times

Granada ®
Granada Publishing ®

To Mary
With all my love
Bill

Tight Corners

Introduction *A word of warning and a word of thanks*

Introduction
A word of warning and a word of thanks

Some of the problems in this book – more than half of them, in fact – are brand-new. Some have been around for years, quite a few for literally thousands of years. Some are wildly fantastic. Some could happen anyday to anybody. Some are so simple you'll be able to crack them straight away. Some are so tricky that they could take hours – if you've got the patience to stay with them that long! But please remember: old or new, tough or easy, weird or straight, they are all only MENTAL exercises, for solving in your head or on paper, *but nowhere else*. Practical experiments with any of them could land you in a dangerous real-life tight corner – and you might not be able to extricate yourself from *that* before disaster struck!

I should like to thank my daughter Carol and Mr Ken Driver, who not only suggested five of the problems, but helped enormously in the planning of this book. Thanks, too, to my son Nigel, Mr Graham Higdon, Mr Nick Jackman and Mr Barnaby Prendergast, all very good people to have beside you when you're in a tight corner for ideas!

Finally, to sum up what this whole book's about, here's a quote from our master sleuth and champion survivor, Dixon Drake. 'Just because no one's lit up an EXIT sign,' he is always saying, with a mocking, daredevil laugh, 'that doesn't mean there's no way out.'

W.V.B.

1 DANGEROUS LEDGE

You're escaping from a gang of dangerous criminals. You climb out on to a window sill, and you can't go back inside because the criminals are all over the house. You are 12 metres from the ground, far too far to jump. Just below the sill, to the left, is a drainpipe. It's clamped firmly to the wall at 2 metre intervals, but there's a snag. The top clamp has come away, so that the drainpipe looks a pretty risky thing to jump on to. Just below you, to the right of the window, is a mass of ivy climbing up the wall of the house, but it's not very thick and you're doubtful if it will bear your weight. You have a length of rope round your waist, and there's a handle on the window behind you, to which you could fasten one end of it. But the rope is only 2.75 metres long. How would you escape?

2   SLIPPERY ROOF

Debbie, a ten-year-old schoolgirl, has an attic bed-room, with a window that is halfway up a tiled, sloping roof. One night, just when she is getting into bed, she hears two cats having a noisy fight in the garden below. Wondering if her pet, Tiswas, is one of the fighters, she leans out of her window too far, and the next thing she knows, she has fallen out of the window and is sliding, slithering and bumping down the sloping roof! She shouts and screams, but her parents are downstairs watching TV and don't hear a sound. Talking of TV, about 1.20 metres above Debbie's head, at the crest of the sloping roof, there is an aerial, with a wire running down the tiles, close to her hand. She manages to clutch hold of this wire, and it slows down her fall. A second later, her feet come up against something solid, and she re-alises it's the gutter at the bottom of the sloping roof.

The gutter, though, is old and rusty. As long as Debbie can hang on to the wire, thus preventing her full weight from pressing on the gutter, she is safe. But at any moment, the wire is likely to snap, and then the gutter won't support her for more than 5 to 10 minutes. It looks as though Debbie, then, is only 7 to 10 minutes away from a very nasty fall. Can anything save her?

3 RICKETY BRIDGE

This is based on a very old circus story. There are no guarantees that it's true, but it's a fascinating story, nonetheless.

Once upon a time there was a world-famous acrobatic and trapeze act called the Pirellos. It consisted of Signor Benito Pirello and his two young sons, Guiseppe (aged 7) and Francisco (aged 9). The Pirellos could perform all kinds of tricks from juggling to tight-rope walking, but their speciality was flying leaps and somersaults.

One day, when the circus was visiting a wild part of Sicily, the Pirellos were kidnapped by bandits, who took them to their lair and bound and gagged them. The bandits' lair was a rocky cave beside a deep ravine. The only way across the ravine was a rickety bridge made of rotting rope. 'Listen to me good,' Pirello had heard the bandit leader say to one of his men. 'Don't ever carry anything heavy over that bridge. If it has to bear a weight of more than 110 kilos, mama mia! It will collapse and drop you into the ravine.'

That night, when the bandits were asleep and snoring loudly, Pirello succeeded in wriggling out of his ropes. He was about to untie Guiseppe and Francisco, but before he could start to do so, the bandit leader woke up.

'You try to escape, huh? For that we kill-a you!'

This put Signor Pirello into a very tight corner indeed. All the bandits were now awake, and brandishing guns. He picked his sons up bodily (they were both still gagged and bound, remember) and rushed out of the cave, with the bandits' bullets pinging all round him. With Guiseppe under one arm and Francisco under the other, he rushed out on to the bridge. He had managed to grab a knife. If he could make it to the other side, and then cut the ropes of the bridge behind him, they would all be safe. But suddenly he remembered that remark of the bandit leader about the bridge collapsing if it had to bear more than 110 kilos. He was 70 kilos; Guiseppe was 25 kilos, and Francisco 30 kilos. He had no time to untie his sons. He obviously couldn't leave either of them behind. But if he tried to carry them both, the bridge would collapse long before they got across.

How could he possibly escape?

The famous detective, Dixon Drake, has been kid-napped by an arch-villain, Maximilian Keen. But Keen, for all his villainy, is a sportsman.

'I will give you one chance to live, Drake,' he says. 'On the table in front of us are two revolvers. One is loaded, the other is not. When I have finished speaking, I shall ask you to choose one of these revolvers, and whichever one you choose will be picked up and fired at your head. If you have picked the loaded revolver, you will obviously die. If you have chosen the unloaded one, I shall consider that you have won this round of our battle, and I promise to let you go free.

'One other thing, my dear Drake. You see my two assistants here? One is called Henreid and the other Rudolf. Henreid has never been known to speak the truth; Rudolf never, ever tells a lie. Before you decide which gun is to be fired at you, I will permit you to ask *one* of my assistants *one* question. And he is under orders to answer.'

Keen starts to chuckle evilly.

'But, I am afraid, I am not going to tell you which is Henreid and which is Rudolf, so you will have no way of knowing whether the answer is the truth or a lie. Mind you, if you are clever enough to think of it, there is a certain way you can put the question which will tell you which is the unloaded gun, in any event. But *are* you clever enough, Drake? That is *my* question.' Keen's chuckle becomes a roar of mock-ing laughter. 'A life-or-death question – for you!'

Can you think of the one way Dixon Drake can put the question so that he will know for certain which is the unloaded gun?

18

5 MONSTROUS MOMENT

This is one of the oldest and most famous stories in the world, so it's quite possible you may happen to know the answer.

People in ancient times, so the story goes, were terrorised by a female monster called Medusa, a creature with wings, claws, enormous teeth and a mass of snakes instead of hair. Medusa was not a beautiful sight, and that is putting it mildly. In fact, anyone who so much as glanced at her face was instantly turned into stone.

The hero Perseus undertook to rid the world of this Medusa, before any more of his friends became statues. He set out in a swift boat, and equipped himself with a sword and a shield. The sword was razor-sharp, and the shield was so highly polished that he could see his face in it.

When he arrived at Medusa's lair, he began to feel sorry that he had been so rash. He dared not look at her but he sensed the monster standing there, staring at him, in what can fairly be called a stony silence. Every second the impulse grew stronger to look up and stare back at that awful face. He knew that would be fatal. How could he defend himself when Medusa pounced on him with those terrible claws? And in any case, how could *he* attack what he couldn't see?

Perseus had a plan. But he had only seconds to put it into action before he was clawed to death or turned to stone. Can you guess what his plan could have been?

Perseus conquered Medusa and cutting off her head with his sword, put it in a bag and slung it over his shoulder. (It had to be in a bag, because even dead,

that terrible face could turn any living thing to stone.)

Perseus was one of the busiest heroes in Greek mythology. He now had to hurry off and rescue the girl he loved, Andromeda, who was in very serious trouble. She had been tied to the rocks on an island called Joppa, and was to be sacrificed to a deadly sea-serpent.

The serpent (sometimes called the Kraken) came out of the sea just as Perseus arrived on the scene. It was so vast that it towered high above the highest hill on the island. It had thick scales that no sword on earth could penetrate; claws that could pierce any shield or piece of armour, and enormous teeth that could chew anyone to pieces in a flash.

Yet Perseus did not hesitate. He knew exactly what he had to do to save Andromeda – and himself – from the clutches of the Kraken. Can you guess what he did?

You have just fallen overboard from a yacht sailing down a river, and you are in dead trouble, because you can't swim a stroke. Somebody throws you a rope-ladder, but the tide in the river is rising at an enormous rate.

The rope-ladder has six rungs, 45 centimetres apart. It takes you two seconds to climb each rung. Meanwhile, the water in the river is rising at 30 centimetres a second.

How can you possibly reach safety before the water is over your head?

8 WELL, WELL, WELL

Here's a rather similar problem. You have fallen down a well, and are splashing about in deep water, with your head about 3 metres below the rim of the well.

You start to try to climb out, but it isn't easy. The well has very slimy, slippery sides, and every time you climb 90 centimetres, you find to your disgust that you fall back 60 centimetres.

Your hands are sore, your nails are broken, and after you have climbed 8.1 metres, and fallen back 5.4 metres, you are too exhausted to climb more than 30 centimetres more.

How can you possibly escape?

9 STAND BY FOR BLASTING!

This is a story from World War II.

An RAF bomber is flying back from a night raid over Germany. It has been badly damaged by anti-aircraft fire, and although it is still manoeuvrable, it cannot climb more than 30 metres above the ground. It is still carrying one massive bomb, and if it drops it from that height, the shock wave coming up from the explosion will blast the plane itself out of the sky!

The trouble is that the bomb flap has been damaged, and is out of the pilot's control. The bomb has already slid half-way out of it, and is on the point of falling.

The plane is nearing the coast, and in thirty seconds' time will be safely over the sea, where a dropped bomb will cause nothing but a harmless splash. But that bomb will be falling in two or three seconds, not thirty. The pilot and the crew have no time, even to escape by parachute.

'Help! We've had it, chaps,' the pilot mutters over the intercom to his crew . . . but then he suddenly realises that if he acts very fast indeed, there is, after all, something he can do.

Can you work out what it is?

You'll only get the answer to this one if you think back carefully to all you know about that most evil of villains, Count Dracula.

The beautiful Lady Caroline Grantleigh has been warned that the Count is in the neighbourhood, and may be coming after her that very night!

'Remember, my dear,' the kindly old Bishop of Transylvania has told her, 'you will be perfectly safe if you keep a crucifix by your bedside, and have a bunch of garlic roots within reach. Vampires cannot pass either of these.' For good measure, her fiancé, the Hon. Archibald Kerr, has lent her his revolver, and shown her how to use it.

That night, before getting into bed, Lady Caroline is sitting in front of her dressing table, combing her beautiful chestnut hair. Suddenly she sees in the mirror a terrifying cloaked figure standing behind her. He is tall and dark, with flashing eyes and teeth.

He glides forwards silently, his hands outstretched towards her neck . . .

'The Count!' Lady Caroline breathes. She reaches out for the revolver, which is on the dressing-table in front of her. But then she remembers that vampires are not harmed by bullets (not ordinary ones, at any rate) and so she looks round for the crucifix and the bunch of garlic. Panic seizes her as she realises that they are both over by the bed – twenty feet away on the far side of the bedroom!

For a moment she almost faints in terror . . . but then suddenly she laughs. Ducking away from those outstretched hands, she turns and faces the intruder boldly.

'My dear sir,' she says coldly. 'Whatever your purpose in coming here, I know now that I have no cause to fear you.'

Can you guess why?

Now for a couple more adventures of that great detective, Dixon Drake.

One night, Drake decided to work late. He walked back to his office, a small room at the top of a building in Hanover Street, London. Everyone else who worked in the building (it contained a lot of offices, belonging to solicitors, insurance firms and so on) had long since gone home. The whole place was deserted, and the corridors were dark and echoing.

Reaching his office, Drake unlocked the door, and clicked on the light – a bright fluorescent strip hanging from the ceiling. Then he walked across to his desk, and was just about to sit down behind it when he heard footsteps in the corridor. The next instance, a man came charging into the room, brandishing a gun. Obviously, thought Drake, the man had been following him, waiting for an opportunity to attack.

His own gun was in the top drawer of the desk in front of him. Instinctively, he reached out to grab it, but the gunman was too quick for him.

'Oh, no you don't, Drake!' he barked, and levelled his revolver at the detective's heart. 'Get away from that desk. Right away. In fact, I want you over by that door, with your back against the wall. And get those hands up higher than a kite, or I'll blast you to kingdom come.'

Dixon Drake was not in the least alarmed.

'Anything to oblige, friend,' he drawled, and carried out all these instructions with great speed – and a secret smile.

The gunman had played into his hands – and he reckoned he could get out of this tight corner in about five seconds flat. Why?

Dixon Drake was always being visited by gunmen.

The next time it happened, it was in his own home. The gunman broke in through a back window without making a sound, and, still moving noiselessly, crept through the house until he reached the door of Drake's study.

This room was furnished with old-fashioned style and elegance. Fine mahogany bookcases lined the walls. There was a large old-style fireplace, with a blazing wood fire in the grate, and in front of it stretched a magnificent scarlet hearthrug, about 2.5 by 1.5 metres. Just to the right of this rug, with his long legs stretching out across it, Dixon Drake himself was lounging in a comfortable leather armchair. He was smoking a curly briar pipe, and looking at peace with himself and all the world. In fact, his eyes were half-closed, and he seemed on the point of dropping off to sleep.

Forgetting that Drake possessed the sharpest pair of eyes in the business, whether they were half-closed or not, the gunman thought he hadn't been noticed. He crept silently across the room until he was standing right in front of the fire, only two or three feet from his intended victim. Then he pointed his revolver at Drake's head, and snarled:

'Stay where you are, and reach for the sky!'

Drake opened his eyes wide, and raised his arms so abruptly that the pipe fell clean out of his mouth and landed at his feet. Lighted tobacco spilled out of it, and the smell of burning filled the air.

'Pick that ruddy thing up and knock it out!' ordered the gunman.

'With pleasure,' drawled Dixon Drake, and the next moment it was the gunman who was in the tight corner.

Can you say why?

It is the year A.D. 2084. Captain Rudd and the crew
of the interplanetary spaceship Zero 444 have landed

on Xerxes, a very small planet far out in the solar system. If you've never heard of it, that's not surprising. It is such a small planet – only about a hundredth the size of Earth – that it was not discovered until A.D. 2050. Zero 444 is the first spaceship ever to go there.

The scientific experts back on Earth have told Captain Rudd and his crew to expect a cold, dark, lifeless world, with a rocky terrain rather like the Moon's. What their telescopes have not revealed is that the rocks on Xerxes are very far from lifeless. They are, in fact, alien beings with very unfriendly feelings towards strangers.

The result is that the moment Rudd (clad, of course, in a spacesuit) steps outside the spaceship he gets the surprise of his life – and it's very nearly the surprise of his death.

A huge rock, weighing at least a ton (1000 kgs) hurls itself forward and lands on top of him.

Three members of his crew leave the spaceship and rush to his rescue, but other rocks, equally heavy, come leaping off the ground and land on top of *them*.

What possible chance have any of them of getting back to the ship alive?

There are some people who make a living out of getting into, and out of, tight corners. The most famous of these escapologists, as they are called, was Harry Houdini.

Houdini certainly earned his fame. On several occasions he had himself strapped in a straitjacket, and left swinging by his feet from the highest point of a skyscraper. At other times, he would have himself buried in a coffin six feet under the ground. Whatever he did, he always escaped without the slightest trouble, partly through skill – and partly through some very clever trickery.

One of his neatest tricks was his way of getting out of solid steel safes.

A week before his travelling magic show would arrive in a town, he would put an advertisement in the local papers, challenging any safe manufacturer in the district to deliver his largest and strongest safe straight to the theatre. This was back in the early days of the century, when many safes could be unlocked from the inside as well as the outside. If a manufacturer happened to send one that couldn't, Houdini's assistants would work on it secretly until it could!

When the performance began, Houdini would walk on to the stage wearing just a pair of bathing trunks. The theatre manager would introduce him, and then bring on a local doctor, if possible somebody well-known to a lot of the people in the audience. This doctor would take Houdini behind the open door of the safe, and examine him to make sure he wasn't concealing a key in his mouth, up his nose, or anywhere else on his body.

Houdini would then shake hands with the doctor and the manager; bow to the audience, and calmly enter the safe. The door would be slammed and locked behind him. A screen would cover the safe.

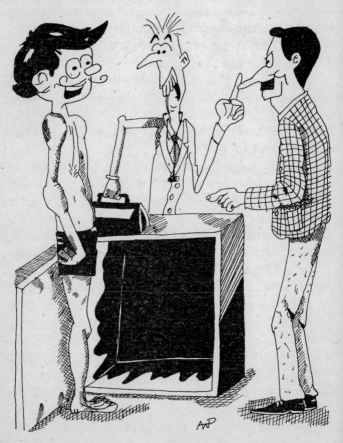

The manager would solemnly warn the audience that the safe only contained enough air to last Houdini for twenty minutes. And the orchestra would play a selection of grim, tense tunes as the minutes ticked by.

Ten. Fifteen. Nineteen. . .

Women in the audience would sometimes scream and faint – but if they'd been watching more closely, they wouldn't have been in the least worried about Houdini's prospects of escaping. Why?

Now that you know the sort of tricks that Houdini got up to, see if you can work out how he performed his most popular stunt.

A huge crowd would assemble by the bank of a river. Some workmen would appear and, in full view of everybody, would hammer together a wooden crate.

Then Houdini would arrive, to loud cheers, wearing, as usual, just a pair of bathing trunks. Still in full view of the crowd, he would be nailed up inside the crate. Very often, he would be handcuffed as well – but then, it never took Houdini more than a minute to get out of any pair of handcuffs ever made.

The crate containing Houdini would then be carried on to a jetty. A tugboat would arrive on the scene, equipped with a crane. The crane would hoist the crate high in the air while the tug steamed out into the middle of the river. Then it would slowly lower the crate until it disappeared beneath the surface of the water.

The crowd held its breath – and wondered if Houdini was doing the same. Only the faintest bubbles showed on the water's surface . . .

Then, again very slowly, the crane would raise the crate. And Houdini would be sitting on top of it, smiling and waving!

The tug would steam back to the bank. Houdini would step ashore, the crowd giving him a hero's welcome. And their cheers would turn to gasps of awe as they were shown the crate – with not a plank or a nail missing from it anywhere.

How do you imagine Houdini had got himself out of his own cunningly-designed tight corner?

Like the stories of Perseus and Medusa, this tight corner comes from the myths of Greece and Rome, and has been told and re-told for more than two thousand years.

I must warn you, it isn't a very pleasant tale. Once again, we have a monster on the scene – not quite as hideous as Medusa, but still not someone you'd like to meet on a dark night. He is a cannibal giant called the Cyclops, an alarming being with only one eye – a huge one, set in the middle of his forehead.

The Cyclops lives on the island of Sicily, tending flocks of sheep, since he evidently likes a spot of lamb when he can't get human fare.

One day, the famous Greek hero Odysseus (leading character of Homer's *Odyssey*) lands on the island, together with his crew. They have with them some coils of rope, some bottles of wine (they got very thirsty, these old heroes) and several sharp swords. With these, they set out against the Cyclops, not realising that the most savage blow with a human sword is just a pinprick to him, and that he can snap the thickest rope as if it were a thread of cotton.

The Cyclops seizes Odysseus and his crew, and eats two crew-members in front of Odysseus's eyes. Then he throws the survivors into what you might call the Cyclopean larder – the cave where he keeps his sheep. There Odysseus and the others have to stay, as helpless as the baa-ing sheep surrounding them, while the Cyclops stands on guard just inside the entrance, glowering at them with his enormous

single eye and obviously trying to decide who to eat next.

Odysseus, though, is not helpless for long. He is one of the wiliest heroes in all mythology. (It was he who thought of the famous Trojan Horse trick to capture Troy – but that's another story.) He remembers the wine which they have brought with them from the ship, and suggests to the Cyclops – probably by gestures – that he might like a drop to wash down all the people he is eating. The monster tries the wine, and likes it so much that he finishes up all the bottles, and becomes totally drunk. Taking a long stick that is lying about in the cave, Odysseus seizes the opportunity to put out the monster's eye.

But he and his party are still in a very tight corner. The blind Cyclops, sober now but in a towering rage, is standing at the entrance and obviously nothing human can pass him without being literally chewed to pieces.

Nothing human . . .

That gives Odysseus an idea so brilliant that it has been remembered for as long as his Trojan horse.

Are you brilliant enough to think of it too?

17   TIME SLIP

Once upon a time – the right words to start this particular story – there lived, in the quaint old Swiss town of Grindelburg, a master clockmaker called Gustav Joachim.

His masterpiece, the great town clock of Grindelburg, could be seen from just about every house and every street in the place. The clock tower was 30 metres high. The clock face measured nearly 9 metres across. Right in the centre of this face (just above where the two hands met) was a little door which Gustav would open whenever one of the two vast clock hands needed repairing.

Sometimes he would take his eleven-year-old son Hans up into the clock tower, and opening the little door, would let the boy peep out at the magnificent view. The peaks of seventeen mountains and the waters of eight lakes could be seen.

Gustav always warned his son: 'Never under any circumstances come up here on your own, my boy.'

Hans would reply 'Jah, jah, father,' but wasn't really listening. He couldn't see why the clock tower should be all that dangerous and was, in fact, dying to explore it on his own.

One night, when Gustav was asleep, Hans stole the clock tower keys from the pocket of the old man's coat, and crept up the winding stairs until he was right behind the clock face. He opened the little door, and stared excitedly out across the silent, sleeping town. But a particularly thick mist had just descended. In an effort to peer through it, Hans leant perilously far out – and just then, the clock chimed half past one. The whole tower shook with the sound – and Hans was shaken clean out of the doorway. He clutched out wildly – and just in time, managed to catch hold of the 4.5 metre-long minute hand, which was of course pointing straight downwards. It was wet and slippery with the clinging mist, and Hans found himself slithering helplessly down it. Fortunately, the hand ended in an arrow, and Hans somehow succeeded in hooking his hands round the arrow bits and hanging on.

He was still in a desperate position, though.

Below him (although he couldn't see it through the mist) was a 30 metre drop straight on to the hard cobblestones of the Grindelburg town square. He was too far up for his cries for help to reach anyone on the ground, even if there had been anyone awake at that hour.

His only chance was somehow to get back to that little door in the centre of the clock face. But how could he possibly do it? Hans was quite strong, and good at climbing along and through things – but the greatest acrobat in the world couldn't have climbed straight up a 4.5 metre clock hand – and a very wet and slippery one at that.

It was all Hans could do to cling on to the end of the hand – and he didn't reckon he could do that for more than another quarter of an hour at the most.

Suddenly Hans had a thought that was so frightening he almost fainted. At the end of that quarter of an hour, the clock would chime again: a three-quarter chime that would shake the tower more violently even than before.

And he was sure it would knock him clean off the slippery hand!

It looks, then, as though Hans is in our toughest tight corner so far – with only 15 minutes to go before a terrifying fall to certain death on the cobblestones of Grindelburg, 30 metres below.

But there is a way out – as time will show.

Here we are, back in the world of mythological monsters. This time, the story comes not from the Greeks or Romans, but from the old Norse myth-makers – the people who recounted the deeds of Odin (or Woden) the Wise and Thor the Thunder God, after whom Wednesday and Thursday are named.

The Norse also told tales about one Sigurd the Dragon Slayer and his most famous victim, Fafnir the Snake Dragon. This Fafnir was a fearsome creature who had slaughtered poor Norse villagers by the thousand. It had no legs, but a long snake-type body that coiled on and on for something like a quarter of a mile. Flames poured from its nose and mouth, so that it could not only wrap itself round you like a boa-constrictor but roast you into a cinder in one second flat.

Fafnir had, though, two weaknesses. Its eyes were set on the top of its head, so that it could see around and above, but not what was happening below. And although it had thick scales all along its back, underneath its skin was soft and could easily be pierced by a sword.

Despite these weaknesses, Sigurd knew that, facing such a creature, he would be in a very tight corner – and might well meet the fate of the thousands of others whom Fafnir had slain. So he thought hard, and took some very sensible precautions.

Fafnir had regular habits, and he knew that the

creature never left its lair until noon. He arrived an
hour before that, and he had with him not only a long,
sharp sword, but a hefty –
What?

Name the implement, and you'll know not only how Sigurd escaped from his tight corner, but also how he slayed the dragon.

Imagine for a moment that you are a mouse. (Well, it makes a change from monsters.) You have been scampering around in the middle of the night in a farmhouse kitchen, and have just fallen into a large jug of full cream milk. You're a strong, healthy mouse, and can probably swim round for an hour or more, but otherwise, your prospects are not bright. The top of the jug is too high, and the sides too smooth, for you to clamber out. The jug itself is too heavy to be toppled over. You are way out of your depth in the milk, and there is no chance of anyone hearing your screams – sorry, squeaks. Can you think of anything that can save you from drowning?

The trouble with being a world-famous detective is that you never know when you are going to be ambushed by arch-villains.

One night, at about 11 o'clock, Dixon Drake was leaving a theatre in the West End of London, and strolling down a back street near Shaftesbury Avenue to the spot where he had parked his car.

Suddenly, four men armed with revolvers emerged from the shadows and surrounded him. He recognised their leader as his old adversary, Maximilian Keen.

'Good evening, Drake', Keen said blandly. 'I suggest you come for a little walk with us.'

Dixon Drake didn't turn a hair.

'I have a better idea, my dear Max,' he drawled. 'I suggest you come for a little run – after me!'

He turned on his heels, and dashed off down the street, ducking and swerving as bullets pinged all round him.

Suddenly he came to the end of the street, and swore under his breath. It was a cul-de-sac – and the only way out, as far as he could see, was a fire escape leading up a tall building on the right.

He dashed on to the fire escape, about 10 metres ahead of his pursuers and ran up flight after flight of clanging iron steps. Finally, breathless and panting hard, he found himself on a roof, ten storeys above Piccadilly. Immediately over his head was an advertising sign, reading HEALTH PRODUCTS LTD in letters of blazing blue, red and gold that lit up the London sky all round him.

'Health Products, eh?' Drake muttered to himself. 'Well, this doesn't seem too healthy a spot to me . . .'

He could hear the footsteps of his pursuers clanging up the last flight of the fire-escape, and hurriedly ducked behind a tall chimney. He had a revolver in his pocket, and three clips of ammunition: eighteen bullets in all. If it came to a shoot-out, he believed he could hold his own for quite a long time. But obviously, not all night. He wished desperately that there was some way in which he could contact his many friends at Scotland Yard, and summon help.

Tantalisingly, Scotland Yard itself was actually in sight. From this high roof, he could make out the building distinctly. It was not more than a mile and a half across London, close by the spires of Westminster Abbey and the mighty tower of Big Ben . . .

If only there was some way of sending a signal –

Drake found himself staring up at the electric sign, and suddenly he had an idea as brilliant as any of the dazzling letters.

Can you say what it could have been?

This is the story of a man who escapes from a very tight corner without ever knowing he is in one!

On a hot summer night, somewhere in the Middle East, two British secret service men, Agents XO5

and XO6, are sitting at a table on the pavement in front of their hotel. Each has a long iced drink in front of him. XO5 has a gin and lime, as a matter of fact, and XO6 a vodka and tonic.

The drinks look very inviting, but in fact, the waiter who has brought them is in the pay of an enemy power, and has just slipped poison into both the glasses.

XO5 feels hot and thirsty. He drinks his gin and lime in a single gulp. XO6 is an altogether cooler type, and sips his vodka and tonic slowly.

Suddenly, XO6 groans and falls off his chair, to lie on the pavement writhing in agony. XO5 rushes off to call a doctor and ambulance . . . wondering if at any moment *he* is going to collapse!

Time goes by. XO6 is rushed to hospital and the doctors save his life only after a grim struggle.

XO5 – to his own astonishment and delight – remains perfectly well!

Yet when the glasses are taken away and examined by the local police, more traces of poison are found in XO5's glass than in XO6's!

Can you explain the luck of XO5?

A famous hero is walking through a wooded stretch of country. Suddenly he falls into a deep pit (around 10 metres deep) which has been specially dug for him by his arch enemy.

Roaring with laughter, the enemy comes up and leans over the pit, to jeer at the trapped hero.

That is a bad mistake on the enemy's part.

'Stay where you are,' the hero commands, from the depth of the pit. 'If you move your head the smallest degree in any direction, you will be dead. And you will be dead, too, if you do not immediately order your men to let down a rope . . .'

Now here's the interesting thing. Our hero has no gun of any kind. He cannot possibly throw a knife up 6-odd metres fast enough to kill his enemy before he has ducked out of sight. And he has no power to hypnotize or cast spells.

Yet the enemy knows he is not bluffing, and can, in fact, do all that he threatens. He does not dare to move his head – and he quickly orders his men to throw down a rope and rescue the hero.

Why?

While we're on the subject of people falling into pits, here is the story of an eighteenth-century magician who called himself Professor Comte.

Not many people remember the good professor now, but the amazing trick that he invented has never been forgotten. You see it performed at every other children's party. Many famous entertainers

have built their whole careers round it. And rarely a week goes by without someone doing it, in one show or another, on TV.

One day, so the story goes, Professor Comte went on a visit to Switzerland. At that time, he had only just invented his amazing trick, and hadn't quite perfected it. Each morning he would take himself off to some remote spot in the Swiss mountains and practise it.

The spot he chose wasn't quite remote enough.

One day, some peasants came by when he was practising and couldn't believe their eyes and ears.

'The man must be a demon!' they told themselves, and before the professor realised what was happening, they had seized him and were dragging him towards a deep lime-kiln that happened to be nearby.

It wasn't until he was on the very edge of the lime-kiln, and staring down into its black, echoing depths, that the professor realised how he could escape.

By performing the trick again, in a different, more dramatic way, he terrified the peasants so much that they ran off into the woods and let him go free.

Can you say what the trick was – without looking up the answer, or waiting until the next time you see (and hear) it on TV?

The first sirens were not wailing alarms on police cars. The word (like so many others) comes from Greek mythology, and originally it was the name of three beautiful but evil sea nymphs.

These sea nymphs were mermaid-like beings who sat on the shores of their rocky island and sang sweet songs to lure passing sailors to their doom.

Their singing had such a hypnotic power that no sailor who heard it could resist turning his ship towards the island, even though it was sure to be wrecked on the rocks, and all aboard drowned.

Only one man heard the cry of the sirens and escaped – and that was our old friend the wily Odysseus, who worked out a way in which he could sail past the island unharmed. Just to be difficult, he scorned to stop up his ears, and could hear the sweet but deadly singing at full blast all the way.

He was not immune to the siren's spell any more than anyone else. As their song filled his ears, he felt a desperate yearning to steer towards the island – and he could not prevent himself first commanding, and then beseeching, his crew to change course and head the sirens' way.

But because of the precautions he had taken, the ship kept sailing straight on by.

Can you work out what those precautions were?

25   DAMP CELLAR

Dixon Drake had fallen into Maximilian Keen's clutches yet again.

When he recovered from the drugged drink his enemy had slipped him, he found he had been locked in a cold, damp cellar.

And 'damp', he soon discovered, was putting it very mildly.

Water was pouring in from somewhere. It was already 30 centimetres high all round him, and was rising at the rate of 15 centimetres every minute!

With difficulty – because they'd handcuffed his wrists behind his back, and also fastened his ankles together with a rope – Drake managed to get to his feet. By the time he'd done so, the water was already lapping around his knees.

Drake didn't like to think about that. Instead, he started studying the only window which the cellar possessed. It was 1 metre square, and he thought he could easily break the glass and climb through it. But there was one snag. The window was 6 metres above the floor – in other words, 4 metres above his head. And there was no furniture in the cellar – no racks, no shelves, nothing he could climb or that would give him a footing, even if he could escape from his bonds.

Drake swallowed hard. The water was now up to the top button of his elegant jacket, and seeping through to ruin his shirt and tie. Suddenly furious, he banged the handcuffs against the wall behind him – and found that he'd done a Houdini: the cuffs sprang open and simply fell off his wrists!

Dixon Drake's bad temper vanished abruptly. In fact, he actually started grinning.

'I'll be out of here in no time,' he drawled to himself, in that mocking tone that had so often reduced Maximilian Keen to fury. 'Or – to be exact – in precisely twenty-eight minutes and a half . . .'

Can you figure out why?

What with sea nymphs and flooding cellars, we seem to have arrived at rather a watery stretch of this book. And while we're about it, here are two more corners that are not only tight – but wet!

Secret Agent XO5 is beginning to believe that for once, his luck has run out. He is on an assignment in a small South American republic called Volizia, and has upset its diabolical dictator, President Andrigos. As a result, he has what seems like the entire Volizian army on his heels.

He is scrambling frantically through some long grass on all fours, with a battalion of soldiers only 100 metres behind him, and machine-gun bullets whistling past his ears at the rate of about a hundred a minute.

Gasping for breath, he flops down amongst some reeds growing beside a very muddy-looking river. The reeds are the hollow kind which you can play a tune on if you put them to your mouth and blow. But XO5 isn't exactly in a mood for musical experiments. He tries to lie low amongst the reeds, but finds to his horror that they are too sparse to give him any real cover.

The soldiers are now less than 50 metres away, advancing in a regular line.

Staccato bursts of machine-gun fire ring out every time they see something suspicious, even if it's only a capybara scurrying through the grass.

In under a minute they'll be reaching the reeds . . .

XO5 realises that he's only got one chance. Making as soft a splash as possible, he jumps into the river, hoping he'll be able to use that vital minute to swim out of sight.

To his horror, he finds that it isn't that sort of river. He finds himself in thick wet mud, only about one metre deep. It's almost impossible to swim in, and suddenly there's no time for swimming anyway. The soldiers are on the bank right behind him.

Any second now, they'll spot him – and there isn't anywhere left to hide.

Or is there?

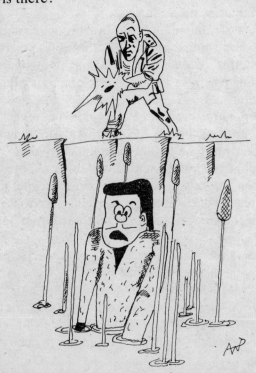

From a shallow stream in sub-tropical Volizia, the scene changes to a deep river somewhere in fog-bound England. And I'm sorry to tell you that you have just landed on the bottom of it, and are in very serious trouble.

You're in the back of a car which has accidentally been driven over the bank in the fog. (Let's say, by a

stupid uncle.) Most modern cars are of such light construction that they would be more likely to float than sink if they plunged into a river. But your uncle's car is a very old model, and it has gone down like a stone.

It is now settling on the bottom, under about 4 metres of water. Through the windows, you can see nothing except swirling weeds, bubbles and perhaps a couple of surprised fish looking in.

An aunt and a cousin are with you in the car, as well as your uncle, and with so many people breathing it in, the oxygen is already getting short.

'Well. It looks as if we've all got to swim for it,' your uncle says brightly, and you try to open the door beside you. But there is so much water pressing on the car from outside that neither it – nor any of the other doors – will budge a centimetre.

By now, you are hot, sweaty, close to suffocating and closer still to panicking.

But *don't* panic. There *is* something you can do to save yourelf and everyone else in the car.

Can you say what it is?

I've some more bad news for you. You have just been kidnapped.

Two ruffians have seized you, gagged you, bound you hand and foot, and thrown you into the back of a small van.

Now it's night, and the van has been driving for hours through unknown countryside. From the speed at which it's travelling, you reckon that at the moment, it must be batting along a motorway.

You are cold, tired, hungry and pretty frightened. Your wrists are red from the chafing ropes and you're sore all over from being bounced about on the floor of the van.

You are sitting facing the rear doors, which are tightly bolted from the outside. Behind you is a wooden screen separating you from your kidnappers, who are in the front of the van, one driving, the other sitting beside the driver.

The only light is a reflection from the van's rear lamps, seeping through at the bottom of the rear door. You can just make out two small cones near the floorboards, which you reckon must be the backs of the rear lamps themselves. You can't see much else, but you can remember from when it was daylight that a tool kit, a jack-handle and a spare wheel are all strapped to the walls of the van somewhere near you.

Not that these can help you much. You're so tightly bound and gagged that there's only one thing you can do – apart from praying, which you're doing all the time anyway. You can bend your knees, and start kicking out.

It's just possible that that might attract someone's attention, although it's a slim chance. The sound will be almost totally drowned by the van's engine, and even if it isn't, who would take any notice of a few

bangs coming from a van in the middle of the night on a motorway?

In the middle of the night on a . . .

Those words suddenly give you an idea, and you know now exactly how to beat the kidnappers and get free.

Don't you?

People get into more tight corners through love than almost anything else, so here, for a complete change, is a little romantic episode.

Let's imagine that you are Romeo, on your way to sneak into Juliet's moonlit garden, where you can stand beneath her balcony and pour out a torrent of passionate words of love.

First, though, you have to climb a very high wall – 7 metres of solid, ivy-covered brick. This is situated about 4 metres in front of Juliet's balcony, which itself is all of 6 metres above the ground.

Fortunately, you just happen to have with you a 7 metre ladder. You lean this against the wall, and climb up.

Next, perched on top of the wall, you swing the ladder over to the garden side, and begin to climb down.

So far, so good. But at that moment, Juliet herself appears on the balcony, and you being Romeo, your heart leaps so violently at the sight of her that you completely lose your footing.

You struggle to regain it – but all you succeed in doing is knocking the ladder, with yourself on top of it, backwards away from the wall.

As you go sailing through the darkness of your beloved's garden, still all you can think about is her beauty. But that isn't going to save you from a very nasty fall.

Can anything save you?

An evil creature, half-man, half-beast, is running amok in London. He has left a trail of havoc down a certain street, smashing windows and beating up everyone he meets – men, women and even chil-

dren. It is known that he has a knife. It is believed he has a gun.

Dozens of policemen arrive on the scene. First, they surround the whole area. Then they take up positions at each end of the street, and slowly march down it, closing in on the monster from both directions at once.

When he sees them coming, the creature suddenly dashes up to the front door of No. 97, which has a brass plate on it. With his maniac strength, he easily forces the door open, and goes inside.

A moment later, the owner of the house appears in the doorway, looking white and shaken.

'I was just coming down the stairs to see what all the fuss was about,' he says, 'when this – this terrible monster charged right past me. I think he's gone right up to the attic, at the top of the house. There's a skylight there, going on to the roof.'

The police rush up to the roof, but there is no sign of the monster there. They search the house from top to bottom, and then do the same to every other house in the street, examining roofs, cellars, gardens and even garden sheds – but they cannot find the slightest trace of him.

Yet the street has been surrounded the whole time with a tight police cordon that no one could have broken through.

Can you say how the monster got away?

If not, here is a clue you might find helpful.

This happened back in Queen Victoria's reign.

A gangster called Johnny Mace has Dixon Drake locked in a room from which there seems no possibility of escape.

It has no windows, and is lit only by a bare electric bulb hanging from the ceiling. The walls are of bleak, bare brick. The only furniture is a small bed, so low that no one can hide underneath. The door is of massive teak which no one could break down.

Drake has been searched, and everything has been removed from his pockets. But he has not, for once, been bound or gagged.

Mace comes to visit his prisoner, with a revolver in his hand. He intends to finish Drake off once and for all. He opens the door, and thinks he sees Drake lying on the bed, fast asleep.

Some arch villains – Maximilian Keen, for instance – would have been too sporting to shoot a sleeping enemy. But not Johnny Mace, the most vicious killer in gangland.

'I sure hope you're having pleasant dreams, punk,' he sneers. 'Because I'm afraid they are your last.'

And he fires, three times, at the figure on the bed.

It does not so much as twitch – and no blood comes out, only a few bits of fluff, a lot of dust, and a feather.

Mace rushes over to the bed – and finds that he has been firing at nothing but a pillow, with Drake's coat wrapped round it to make it look like a body.

As for the great detective himself, there is no sign of him, anywhere in the room.

Can you work out how he has got away?

Secret Agent XO5 is on the run again.

This time he has a gang of five enemy agents on his heels, but at least he is not in a hostile country. He is running, late at night, through the deserted streets of a Thames-side town south of London.

Bullets, though, are just as unpleasant in England as anywhere else, and XO5 is just as anxious to shake off these five agents as he was to evade the Volizian army. Finding that they are catching up on him, he leaps over some iron railings into the grounds of a famous historic building. Unfortunately, they are pretty good at getting over railings too, and soon all five are once again close behind him.

Not that XO5 is by any means beaten yet. He heads for one corner of those historic grounds, where there is what looks like an enclosed garden, about 100 metres square, and surrounded by a 2 metre hedge.

There are two gates in this hedge, about six metres apart.

XO5 rushes through the first gate, with the five enemy agents still following, their bullets whizzing round him.

Two minutes later, XO5 comes running out through the second gate, and makes off across the grounds. But even after ten minutes have passed, none of the foreign agents has reappeared.

Yet XO5 has no weapon on him – and in any case, could hardly have shot or knocked out five men in two minutes flat.

So what *has* been happening behind the hedge?

33 JUST OUT OF REACH

Now let's suppose that *you're* on the run from a gang of five enemy agents. You have led them up on to a roof, but now you're stuck.

The only way forward is to clamber up on to an adjacent roof, but it's 4 metres higher than the one on which you're standing. You are, let's say, a rather short agent – about 1.65 metres – and even with your arms fully extended, can only reach up about 2.40 metres. You can jump, say, another 75 centimetres, but that still isn't enough to let you get your fingers over the top of that adjoining roof.

While you're struggling vainly to do so, your enemies start to catch up on you. Two of them seize you, and pull you to the ground. There is a struggle, during which (being pretty handy with your fists) you knock them both unconscious. But by now, you can hear the other three climbing up the fire-escape to the roof. You remember that one of them – Mario – is a crack shot with a revolver. (You lost your own gun during the chase.)

You reckon you have twenty seconds at the most to get on to that adjacent roof before these three launch their attack, and Mario's bullets start whizzing your way . . .

But however desperate the situation, that roof is still 4 metres above you, and you are still only 1.65 metres tall.

So what can you possibly do?

Now for an 'on-the-run' story – on wheels.

An 11-year-old boy named Paul has made an enemy of a tough mob, who lie in wait for him outside the gates of his school.

He knows that they are going to be there, but he has a bicycle, and they are on foot, and so he reckons he can flash past them and get away.

Unfortunately, he's forgotten that there's a steep hill just outside the school, and this slows him down so much that the mob almost catches up with him.

Then, just a metre or so from the top of the hill, with the gang leader only about 3 metres behind him, Paul hits real trouble.

The chain falls clean off his bike.

The wheels don't respond to the pedals, and worse than that, actually start going backwards, taking him downhill towards his enemies. He tries to brake, but the brake-pads are worn, and only slow down the bike.

There are now only 2 metres between him and the mob, and he's slithering back at a rate of at least a metre a second. The mob are running forward at a rate of at least twice that. In a second or less, then, Paul will be amongst his enemies, falling off a useless bike, and completely in their power.

How can he possibly get away?

You are the heroine of a very old-fashioned thriller, and a very old-fashioned villain – a moustached type who has to be called Jasper – has just tied you to a railway line.

There you are, lying flat on your back on the sleepers between two massive iron rails. Ropes have been passed around your left wrist and ankle, fastening them to the side of the rail on your left, and your right wrist and ankle have been firmly roped, in the same way, to the side of the rail on your right.

The train – an old-fashioned one, of course, with a powerful steam engine in front – is roaring relentlessly towards you.

You struggle hard to break the ropes, but they all hold fast. You hope desperately that some hero will appear in the nick of time to rescue you, but no one comes.

You scream at the top of your voice – but the thunder of the approaching train completely drowns the sound. And suddenly your eyes, nose and throat are filled with steam; the world goes dark, and you realise to your depthless horror that *the train is on top of you*!

If you think I've gone too far this time – that there's no possible way anyone could get out of that! – perhaps you'd like a couple of very small clues.

Jasper hasn't been reading his villain's handbook carefully enough. Either that, or he isn't really such a bad chap after all . . .

Here's another story from the age of steam.

Dixon Drake (just at the beginning of his long and successful career) is being chased by a gang of hoodlums along a railway line, about a hundred metres past a small country station.

In a desperate attempt to get away, Drake climbs the 'iron ladder at the side of a tall railway signal. From the top of this, he thinks, he might be able to jump on to the roof of a passing train. However, he loses his footing and the next thing he knows, he is dangling from the signal arm, which happens to be horizontal – in other words, in the STOP position.

Below him is a drop of ten metres on to the railway line, and as if that isn't enough, the gang of hoodlums are waiting for him along the track, their guns at the ready. The leader of the gang has hustled down the track to the signal box; has held up the signalman, and commanded him to pull the lever marked 'GO'. If the signal arm drops, Drake will obviously not be able to help sliding off.

Just to add to the fun, a train is waiting at the station with steam up, ready to go the moment the signal changes. It is facing in Drake's direction, so when the great detective falls, he will find himself right in the path of the oncoming train. The engine, incidentally, has a low guard in front of it, which will make mincemeat of Drake even if he lies flat between the rails.

The signal-box lever is working perfectly. The train will start the moment the signal changes.

How can Drake possibly survive?

Clue (which will really only make sense to railway buffs, but might put some others on the right track, if they think about it); this railway was in the South of England. There would be no hope for Drake if it was in the West.

37 LONG DROP

It's your first parachute drop. You have just jumped out of the plane. You have counted slowly to ten – just as the instructor said – but your parachute hasn't opened. You are dropping like a stone, with nothing between you and the hard, hard ground but 1,600 metres of air. What can you possibly do?

'Shiver my timbers,' as they used to say in the old sea stories, we haven't had a yarn about smuggling yet. So heave-ho, my hearties, and stand by for the tale of old Tom Oakley, the last in a long line of Cornish smugglers, who one dark November night found himself in the tightest corner of his crooked career.

The first part of the operation had gone so smoothly, too. At 1 a.m. old Tom had set out from the smuggling gang's secret headquarters, Crossbones Cove, a desolate spot on a wild and rocky stretch of the Cornish coast. As planned, he had taken his battered old motor boat, the *Mary Lou*, five miles out to sea, where he had contacted a foreign steamer and taken aboard six large crates of smuggled brandy. Again as planned, he had turned the motor boat round and headed back towards Crossbones Cove, where the gang were waiting to help him unload the brandy. (After that, the plan was that he should go back for another load, and carry on fetching smuggled brandy from ship to shore for the rest of the night.) But when the *Mary Lou* was still about a mile out from the cove, Tom saw someone waving a red lantern. That was the gang's emergency signal. It meant: 'Keep away. Coastguards about.'

So instead of going towards the shore, Tom drove the *Mary Lou* round and round in circles, waiting for a signal from a green lantern, which would mean that the coast was clear. Minute after minute, and finally more than an hour went by, but that signal never came – for the simple reason that the coastguards had arrested the whole gang, and there was no one left in the cove to send it!

When at last he tired of waiting, and decided to head for the cove no matter what the risk, old Tom got the shock of his life. The engine – an ancient four-stroke motor dating back to pre-war days – gave a spluttering 'putt-putt' and then packed up.

Tom swallowed hard, and found himself bitterly regretting that he had ever embarked on the smuggling game. He was more than a mile from the shore, in very deep water. A wind had come up, and the sea was pretty rough. Worse, a strong tide was sweeping the *Mary Lou* straight towards the Skull's Teeth, the deadliest rocks on that entire coast!

There was no lifebelt or life-jacket aboard the *Mary Lou*. (Tom had chucked them out before he'd started, to make as much room as possible for the crates.) Since smugglers' boats are intended to slip through the darkness unseen, there were no lamps on board either, so there was no way he could signal for help. And although Tom wasn't a bad swimmer, he was getting on in years, and he knew he wouldn't have a chance against that powerful tide.

He tried to shout for help, but realised he was wasting his breath. There was nobody within earshot, and in any case, the whistling wind was whipping his words away into the darkness the instant they left his mouth. Breathless, freezing and very, very scared, Tom made one last forlorn attempt to start the engine. This time, it didn't even produce a single 'putt' – only a faint, dry, tinkling noise that sounded like 'plink plank plink'.

Old Tom started so violently that he nearly fell overboard. It was almost as if the *Mary Lou* was talking to him, and telling him to '*think, man, think!*'

Despite the numbing cold, and his equally numbing fear, he suddenly realized how he could get himself and the *Mary Lou* to safety.

Can you plink – er, that is, think – what it was?

Just once more, let's go back to the myths of Greece and Rome – and meet another monster.

This one was called the Minotaur, and lived on the island of Crete, down dozens of winding corridors in a huge, maze-like underground lair known as the Labyrinth.

The Minotaur had a bull's head, a man's body, and the appetite of a ravenous giant. Every so often, the King of Crete had to send human victims into the Labyrinth as a feast for the beast. And he usually sent no less than fourteen at a time – seven young men and seven girls. If he didn't, the Minotaur would go roaring round and round the corridors of the Labyrinth, shaking the whole island like a rumbling volcano.

One day, the Greek hero Theseus arrived in Crete, and asked the King if he could be included amongst the next batch of Minotaur victims. He did not intend, of course, to let himself be eaten, but was hoping to fight and slay the monster. The King's daughter, a clever and beautiful maiden called Ariadne, fell in love with Theseus on sight, and was very worried about what he was planning to do. She had spent all her life in her father's palace on the edge of the Labyrinth, and had seen far too many brave young men and girls disappear into its black depths, never to be seen again.

'Don't you realise,' she asked the hero, 'that no ordinary sword would be the slightest use against that fearful beast? And even if you do kill it without help, you will never, never find your way out of the Labyrinth.'

'But I have given my solemn oath that I will join the victims,' Theseus replied. 'I cannot go back on it now. What can I do?'

'Take these,' said Ariadne. And she gave him two presents. One was a special sword belonging to her father, which was so sharp and strong that it enabled Theseus to kill the Minotaur with ease.

The second gift came in handy after the battle, when he and the thirteen other 'victims' found themselves in the total blackness of the Labyrinth, with winding corridors stretching out all round them, and (as Dixon Drake would have put it) not an EXIT sign in sight!

But then, that second present of Ariadne's was, in its way, a kind of EXIT sign, and led them straight to freedom.

Can you guess what it could have been?

This time, the whole population of Greater London is in a tight corner – in fact, in peril of their lives.

Maximilian Keen, in the most terrible plot of his long arch-villainous career, has hidden a monster nuclear device somewhere in the tower of Big Ben.

The device has a microphone attachment, and is set to go off the moment the mike picks up the first stroke of midnight reverberating around the tower.

Dixon Drake uncovers the plot just in the nick of time, and arrives at the tower to dismantle the bomb at precisely five minutes to twelve. The trouble is, he does not know precisely where the device is hidden. He decides that it could either be right up inside the big bell at the top of the tower, or hidden under the floorboards of a room on the ground floor, just inside the entrance.

Since he can't be in two places at once, he has brought with him a man on loan from the British Secret Service, who has had experience of bomb disposal work in the past. This man turns out to be (surprise, surprise!) none other than Secret Agent XO5.

There is not a moment to lose. XO5 starts to pull up the floorboards in the ground-floor room. Drake takes the lift to the top of the tower, which is so high that it is 11.58 p.m. before he arrives. He rushes into the room that houses the great, 13-stone (that is around 83 kilos) bell, peers up into it, and groans. There is no sign of any nuclear device there.

He has a two-way radio, and hurriedly contacts XO5 down below.

'Any luck your end, old chap?' he drawls.

'Yes.' XO5's voice is so tense that it is little more than a hoarse rasp. 'Yes. I've found the bomb all right, D.D. – and the mike that will trigger it off. All I've got to do is snip this little bit of wire between the bomb and the mike. And I've got the cutters out now . . .'

Drake looks at his watch, and suddenly his voice becomes equally hoarse and strained.

'Sure you can do it in time? You haven't got much. I make it 11.59 and twenty seconds.'

'I should have long enough,' says XO5. Then his gasp of horror sends a crackle down the two-way radio. 'Oh, hell, that's torn it . . . The cutters have just slipped out of my hand – and they've fallen under the bomb. Got to – got to be careful how I pick them up. If I jolt anything–'

'Don't talk, man. Get to work – and make it fast.'

At that very moment, above Drake's head, the huge clock begins to chime – the full four-quarter chime that precedes the first stroke of midnight.

Ding dong ding dong . . . Ding dong ding dong . . . Ding –

The sound sets Drake's head ringing as violently as if his skull itself had become a bell. But more shattering still is the thought that there are now only three seconds left to save London.

And suddenly – *dong ding dong* – those seconds, too, have gone!

In the last, breathless moment between the last chime and the first, fateful *boom*, the two-way radio crackles into life.

'Okay, D.D.. I've picked up the cutters now,' says XO5. 'I'm just going to snip–'

For Drake, the rest of his sentence is drowned in an earth-shattering roar of sound as the great bell chimes the first stroke of twelve.

And the microphone on the bomb has not been cut off. The bomb will have been triggered . . . and any second he, XO5, Big Ben and all Greater London will vanish in a vast holocaust of heat and flame!

So thinks Dixon Drake.

But, in this moment of near-total terror, the great detective has for once got his reasoning very slightly wrong.

Can you say why – and get London out of the tightest corner of them all?

Exits
– in other words, the answers

1 DANGEROUS LEDGE

The drainpipe isn't safe to jump on to from the window sill, because its top clamp has come away from the wall. But it's perfectly safe 2 metres further down, where it *is* firmly clamped, as the picture shows. And with a 2.5 metre length of rope, you could easily climb down 2 metres, then swing across, clutch the pipe, and go down it safely to the ground. (Don't forget this is just a problem on paper. Real-life drainpipes are often far from safe, whether clamped or otherwise.)

2 SLIPPERY ROOF

Can anything save Debbie? Yes, her parents can, for a start. They're downstairs watching TV, remember, and when the wire from the aerial snaps, their set is going to go bananas. Let's hope they will rush out into the garden and look up at the aerial – and then of course, they'll see Debbie's plight. The gutter will hold her weight for 5–10 minutes, giving them plenty of time to rush up to her bedroom, lean out of the window, and pull her safely back inside.

3 RICKETY BRIDGE

Signor Pirello is an expert acrobat, with an acrobat's strong arms. His sons are also acrobats, and accustomed to flying and somersaulting through the air. As he crosses the bridge, Pirello throws first one son up in the air, and then the other. He is careful always to throw one up a split second before the other lands, so that the weight on the

101

bridge is never more than his own weight plus Guiseppe's (totalling 95 kilos) or his own weight plus Francisco's (totalling 100 kilos).

4 LIFE-OR-DEATH QUESTION

Drake has to ask one of the assistants *which the other assistant would say is the loaded gun*. Why? Because if the assistant he has asked is the truthful Rudolf, he will tell him truthfully how Henreid would have replied. But Henreid is a liar, so this answer will be a lie. On the other hand, if the assistant he has asked is the lying Henreid, he will obviously lie about how the truthful Rudolf would have replied. So this answer, too, will be the wrong one. All Drake has to do is choose the other gun from the one named, and he can be sure that he has picked the unloaded one. That is, of course, as long as Maximilian Keen was telling the truth!

5 MONSTROUS MOMENT

Perseus charged forward, swinging his sword, and with one blow, struck off Medusa's head. How could he see to do it? He looked at the monster's reflection in his highly-polished shield. No one said anything about the *reflection* of Medusa's face having the power to turn victims to stone.

6 ANOTHER MONSTROUS MOMENT

As you can see from the illustration, Perseus still had Medusa's head in a bag slung over his shoulder. Even dead, remember, that head could turn any living thing to stone . . . and that certainly included Krakens! (By the way, there are various versions of this story. I have followed the one used in the recent film *Clash of the Titans*. If you went to that film, you'll have seen a really terrifying Medusa's head, turning, with one flash from its green eyes, a still more terrifying Kraken to stone.)

102

7   RISING TIDE
The water will *never* rise over your head – because the yacht is floating on the river and as the water-level rises the yacht will, of course, rise with it, taking the rope-ladder up too.

8   WELL, WELL, WELL
Thirty centimetres is all you *need* to climb – because it will take you to the rim of the well, and you'll be clambering out, not slithering back down a slippery wall!

9   STAND BY FOR BLASTING!
The plane cannot climb, but it is manoeuvrable in other ways – so there's nothing to prevent the pilot flying it *upside down* for 30 seconds, thus stopping the bomb slipping any further through the flap until the plane is over the sea.

10   FOR DRACULA FANS ONLY
Lady Caroline has remembered that vampires can never be reflected in mirrors. Therefore her caller cannot be Count Dracula, but must be either a thief or someone playing a grim joke on her. In either case, he is human – and that gun is a real protection after all. So Lady Caroline is not bluffing: she really has 'no cause to fear'.

11   'STICK 'EM UP!' – 1
The light switch is just beside the door. (Drake clicked on the light immediately after unlocking it, remember.) And the gunman has just commanded Drake to stand 'over by that door, with your back against the wall' – in other words, right in front of the switch! All he has to do is lean back heavily against the switch, and the room will be plunged into darkness . . . during which a master-sleuth like Drake will have no trouble turning the tables on his opponent at all.

103

12 'STICK 'EM UP!' – 2

Stooping to pick up the pipe, Drake catches hold of the hearthrug and pulls it clean out from under the gunman's feet! The gunman falls over backwards, and, of course, before he has picked himself up, Drake has grabbed his gun . . .

13 PLANET OF THE ROCKS

They have quite a good chance, really. A planet only 100th the size of Earth, provided it had the same density as Earth, would only have 100th of our gravity – and everything would weigh only 100th of what it does here. So a ton of rock would really only weigh a little more than 10 kgs – the weight, say, of a rather large dog. Not something to pin tough astronauts down for long!

14 HOUDINI PLAYS IT SAFE

The key had been slipped to Houdini by the manager who, remember, shook hands with him *after* the doctor had finished his examination, but before he stepped into the safe.

15 HOUDINI IN THE RIVER

Houdini had a pair of wire-cutters, perhaps even a small hammer, concealed in his trunks. (No doctor searched him on this occasion!) He started work on the crate the moment he was inside it – and it was kept in the air for quite a long while before being lowered into the river. During this time, Houdini weakened the nails on the crate by nipping off their ends with the cutters, or hammering them out of the crate from the inside. After that, when he was in the water, he could easily prise a couple of planks off the top of the crate and clamber out. No one would see he'd prised them away – because when he broke surface he was sitting on the crate! And his assistants would hastily hammer them back into place while the tug-boat was steaming back to the bank. By that time, the crowd was far too busy cheering Houdini to hear the noise, or notice that the crate was momentarily out of their sight!

16   ONE IN THE EYE FOR CYCLOPS
The cave, remember, was full of the Cyclops's sheep – and Odysseus has with him several coils of rope (brought from the boat, along with the wine.) He ties the sheep together in threes, and under each trio of sheep he hides one of his companions. (The men hang upside down, clinging to the wool on the underside of the sheep.) When the sheep are driven past the blind Cyclops, all the giant's hands encounter is wool. Odysseus and all his friends escape, and the first the Cyclops knows about it is when he hears the hero's mocking laugh ringing across the island – as he sails away over the sea.

17   TIME SLIP
It's impossible to climb *up* the long, slippery minute hand – but it shouldn't be difficult for an agile lad like Hans to climb *along* it. And that's just what he'll be able to do – because the hand, pointing at a quarter to two instead of half past one, will be horizontal not vertical. And if he starts his climb at, say, 1.43, when the hand is almost horizontal, he should be back through the little door before the first chime.

18   SIGURD AND THE SNAKE-DRAGON
Sigurd's 'secret weapon' was a hefty spade, with which he dug a ditch outside the dragon's lair. Then he crouched in the ditch, sword at the ready. Since the dragon could not look down, it slid straight on over the ditch. All Sigurd had to do was wait until its heart (or some other vital part) was overhead, and then stab upwards. The dragon's skin, remember, was soft underneath.

19 MOUSADVENTURE

I have it on the authority of several farming friends that a mouse swimming round for long enough in a jug of full-cream milk would churn it in to butter. In which case, it might get smothered, but certainly wouldn't drown. And once the surface of the butter was firm, it could very probably jump clean out of the jug, having had, you might say, a very narrow squeak.

20 SIGN FROM THE SKY

Drake shot out the eleven letters A, T, H, R, O, U, C, T, S, L and T, leaving the message: '*HELP – D.D.*' He still had seven bullets left with which to keep Maximilian Keen & Co at bay.

21 THE LUCK OF XO5

The poison was in the ice. By gulping his drink, XO5 gave his ice cube no time to melt and release the poison. But of course, it *had* melted by the time the police examined the glasses. Which is why XO5's glass was found to have more poison in it than XO6's.

22 THE POWER OF A HERO

As you might have guessed from the rather stilted way the hero speaks, this is not a modern story. The 'famous hero walking through a wooded stretch of country' is actually Robin Hood taking a stroll through Sherwood Forest. Naturally, he had his bow and arrows with him when he fell into that pit, and his enemy (the Sheriff of Nottingham, who else?) knows that if he doesn't do exactly what Robin says, he will get a swift arrow in the neck from the finest archer in all England. No wonder he doesn't dare to take the risk!

23 THE AMAZING NEW TRICK

Professor Comte was the world's first ventriloquist. When the peasants first saw him, he was probably practising with a doll. But he used much more dramatic voice-throwing to escape from their clutches. He made a deep voice come thundering out of the kiln, roaring: '*Let him go!*' – and they hastily did.

24 SIREN SONG

Odysseus had ordered his crew to bind him fast to the mast – and then to stop up their ears with wax. So however much he wanted to respond to the sirens' call, he could not do anything himself – and however loudly he shouted to the crew, they couldn't hear a word he said. In fact, they thought he was urging them to lash him still more firmly to the mast – and did just that!

25 DAMP CELLAR

Now that he had broken out of his handcuffs, Drake could soon free his legs, and then start swimming! The rising water was at present around his chest (about 1.50 metres off the floor). So in 28 minutes, it would have taken him up to the level of the window, 6 metres above the floor. The other half-minute would allow Drake time to break through the window, and scramble out, free.

26 NOWHERE TO HIDE?

Yes, there is a place XO5 can hide. He can lie down flat on his back in the 1 metre-thick mud, using one of the hollow reeds to breathe through. He should be quite unnoticed by the army – just as long as he doesn't accidentally start playing a tune!

27 SUDDENLY YOU'RE SUNK

It may sound crazy, but the answer is to wind down a window and let the water flood in. In seconds, the water pressure inside the car will balance the pressure outside, and the doors can then be opened. Believe it or not, this is a tight corner that quite a few people have actually been in – and survived, by the method described.

28 NOW YOU'RE KIDNAPPED

The jack-handle, tool-kit and spare wheel were just mentioned to confuse you. The thing to concentrate on is the rear lights. The cones containing their 'works' are within reach of your feet – and if you kick against them you should pretty soon put them out of action. The kidnappers won't hear – the roar of the engine will drown your kicking. And on a motorway at night, the police are very hot indeed on people driving without rear lights. They will soon be stopping the van – and all you have to do then is kick out again to let them know you're there.

29 ALAS, POOR ROMEO

Something certainly can save Romeo. The ladder is 7 metres long and falling towards the garden – with Juliet's 6 metre balcony only 4 metres away. So the top of the ladder would actually fetch up on the balcony itself, and Romeo's sail through the air will end with him falling right into his beloved's arms. Well, I said this was a romantic episode!

30 VANISHING MONSTER

The plate read 'Dr Henry Jekyll'. Now that you know the house-owner's identity, I don't think I need tell you what happened to the monster, who was, of course, none other than Mr Hyde.

31 VANISHING DETECTIVE

Drake was hiding behind the door, and slipped out of the room soundlessly while Mace was examining the 'body' on the bed.

32 VANISHING AGENTS

XO5 has led his enemies into the grounds of Hampton Court, in Surrey, where there is a famous maze. Clearly, they all got lost in there – except for XO5, who must have known the quick way out!

33 JUST OUT OF REACH

Don't forget those two enemies you have knocked out. Put them on top of each other, and use them as a springboard. That should easily give you the extra ½ metre you need. In fact, if he was fat enough, one man would do . . .

34 THE BACKWARD BIKE

Paul would certainly be in dead trouble – if he wasn't so near the top of the hill. As it is, he's only got to jump off his bike, and push it for a few seconds. Then he'll be over the top, and be able to freewheel down the other side, clean away from the mob. (There's nothing to stop a chainless bike freewheeling – very fast indeed.)

35 HARD LINES

Most probably, Jasper is in love with you, and doesn't want to harm you – merely to scare you into accepting his next dastardly proposal of marriage! Otherwise, he would have tied you across the lines, not between them. And he wouldn't have so carefully fastened your wrists and ankles alongside the rails, instead of on top of them. As things are, the train will pass straight over your body without touching it. (There must be enough room. It's already on top of you, and you haven't felt a thing!) The only thing it will actually touch will be the ropes, crushing them to atoms, and setting your wrists and ankles free!

36 MORE TROUBLE ON THE RAILWAYS
Yes, you've guessed it. Types of signal varied from
railway to railway, and still do, from region to region of
British Rail. In the South, I'm told, they go *up*, not down,
when they change to 'GO'. So Drake won't fall – he'll
rise. And he should be able to hang on to the upward
sloping arm for a lot longer than a downward sloping one.
In a second, anyway, the train will be going past, and
jumping down on its roof, he can wave the gang goodbye.

37 LONG DROP
Pull the ripcord, of course – as you forgot to do when
you'd counted ten!

38 SMUGGLER AT SEA
Most petrol engines (and certainly all pre-war ones) can
run, in an emergency, on a lot of things besides petrol –
methylated spirits, vodka, whisky and certainly brandy!
So all old Tom had to do was kick open a crate and pour a
bottleful of smuggled brandy into the fuel tank and the
engine would have spluttered into life and seen him safely
ashore. The coastguards would probably have been
watching for him and would have arrested him as soon as
he arrived. But perhaps they'd have decided that he'd
learnt his lesson.

39 THE WAY-OUT GIFT
Ariadne had given Theseus a large ball of twine, which he
unwound behind him all the time that he was going into
the Labyrinth. Following the twine, of course, enabled
him and his fellow-victims to find their way out of the
Labyrinth again.

40 THE STROKE OF TWELVE
Dixon Drake, up in the bell tower of Big Ben, would hear
the stroke instantly. But the sound will take a split second

to travel down that high tower to the ground. If, during that split second, XO5 clips the wire, then the microphone will never pick up the sound, the bomb will not be triggered – and London will survive.